AFRICAN-AMERICAN HISTORY

AFRICAN-AMERICAN CULTURE

by Darice Bailer

Content Consultant
Ibram X. Kendi, PhD
Assistant Professor, Africana Studies Department
University at Albany, SUNY

Core Library

An Imprint of Abdo Publishing
www.abdopublishing.com

Published by Abdo Publishing, a division of ABDO, PO Box 398166, Minneapolis, Minnesota 55439. Copyright © 2015 by Abdo Consulting Group, Inc. International copyrights reserved in all countries. No part of this book may be reproduced in any form without written permission from the publisher. Core Library™ is a trademark and logo of Abdo Publishing.

Printed in the United States of America,
North Mankato, Minnesota
022014
092014

Editor: Holly Saari
Series Designer: Becky Daum

Library of Congress Cataloging-in-Publication Data
Bailer, Darice.
  African-American culture / by Darice Bailer.
      pages cm. -- (African-American history)
  Includes index.
  ISBN 978-1-62403-143-4
1. African Americans--Social life and customs--Juvenile literature.
2. African Americans in literature--Juvenile literature. 3. African Americans--History--Juvenile literature. I. Title.
  E185.86.B247 2014
  305.896'073--dc23
                        2014000105

Photo Credits: Gary He/AP Images, cover, 1; North Wind/North Wind Picture Archives, 4, 6, 10, 24; Frank Wiese/AP Images, 14; Red Line Editorial, 15, 30; Chuck Burton/AP Images, 16; Carl Van Vechten/Library of Congress, 21; Keith Jenkins/AP Images, 26; Werner Kreusch/AP Images, 28, 45; Julio Cortez/AP Images, 31; John D. Kisch/Separate Cinema Archive, 34; New Line Cinema/AP Images, 37; AP Images, 38; Doug Mills/AP Images, 40

CONTENTS

CHAPTER ONE

SHARING AND SPREADING CULTURE

In 1619 the first African slaves arrived in the British colonies of the present-day United States. The slaves were forced to work for no pay for white colonists. Most slaves worked in the South. They worked in fields under the hot sun all day. White people owned the slaves. Slaves were considered property. They had no rights and had to do what their

When Africans were forced to come to America, they brought their culture with them.

Despite lack of freedom, slaves were sometimes able to gather to tell stories and take part in their traditions.

masters said. The slaves could be whipped if they did not obey.

Africans Bring Culture

Africans from many different parts of Africa brought their different cultures with them from their homelands. Culture includes people's traditions, music, art, religion, and beliefs. Culture helps express who people are and the way they live. Culture is how people speak and use words. Culture helps people learn about the past to understand who they are today. Africans brought these things to their new lives in North America.

Schomburg Center for Research in Black Culture

The Schomburg Center for Research in Black Culture is part of the New York Public Library. It is one of the best places to research African-American culture and history. For more than 80 years, the center has collected materials about African-American life in the United States. The center hosts photographs and writings of many important African-American actors, musicians, artists, and political figures. The center also offers programs and events to teach African-American history and culture.

Slave masters did not want slaves to hold on to their African culture. This was one way they tried to control slaves. They were not very successful though. Slaves had little else to hold on to from their homes in Africa. So keeping their culture strong was very important. Most slaves were not allowed to read or write. So they prayed, danced, and sang the way they had in Africa.

Soul Food

During the time of slavery, owners fed African Americans food the masters did not want. Slaves baked bread for their masters. They were given the crust to eat themselves. They carved meat for their owners and were given the skin. Cooks seasoned the scraps with onions, garlic, and thyme. The food became part of their culture. Some foods that are popular with African Americans today stem from this southern past. Two examples are fried chicken and biscuits.

Today's African-American Culture

Slavery was outlawed in the United States in 1865. Slaves were now free.

EXPLORE ONLINE

The focus in this chapter is how African culture has influenced African-American culture. The website below discusses key areas of African-American culture today. As you know, every source is different. How is the information given in the website different from the information in this book? What information is the same? How do the two sources present information differently? What can you learn from this website?

Black Culture Connection
www.mycorelibrary.com/african-american-culture

But hard times were far from over. They continued to pass on their culture to their children. African culture mixed with other cultures in America to form a unique African-American culture. Many aspects of African-American culture today hold African roots. These include music, folktales, and religion.

RELIGION

Religion is the soul of African-American culture. Before coming to America, Africans took part in their unique religions in different parts of the country. Many worshipped a type of God. Often, the God was a creator and ruler of heaven and Earth. One way Africans worshipped was by dancing and singing. Drummers played in the center of a group of people. Listeners moved their heads and shoulders.

Slaves gathered together to worship on a regular basis.

Call and Response

In many parts of Africa, calling out to villagers was a way Africans greeted each other. A person would call out a greeting. The other person would call out a response. Africans also shared important news this way. Slaves began calling out to each other in America as well. This call and response was the foundation of African-American music and worship.

They rocked and swayed to the sound of the beat. They clapped their hands and stamped their feet. They sang in their native languages, then later in English.

In America white slave masters often did not allow slaves to practice their religion. So slaves adjusted. They met in a forest and worshipped while hidden behind trees. They shouted, sang, and prayed the way they had back in Africa.

Spirituals

In America slaves began embracing Christianity. Christians worshipped a God who was similar to theirs back home. Most African Americans became Christians. They blended African music with Christian hymns. These songs became known as spirituals. The singers clapped their hands in front of them or on their knees. They stamped their feet, swayed back and forth, shouted, and sobbed. This became known as shout worship. It became popular in African-American churches.

Gospel

From about 1896 to 1920, gospel hymns began replacing spirituals in religious music. Gospel hymns were songs of hope. The songs brought joy to African Americans who sang them. African Americans faced racism and segregation. Times were hard. But the music lifted them up. The songs told them the Lord would

Kwanzaa

Kwanzaa is a holiday that celebrates African culture. The first Kwanzaa was in 1966. The holiday begins the day after Christmas. It lasts seven days. It celebrates the harvest in Africa. Families light candles every night. A black candle stands for people who have come from Africa. It is lit first. The next candles are red. They stand for the struggle African Americans have faced. The last candles are green. They stand for hope.

Gospel music is an important aspect of African-American religion.

take care of them. Men and women clapped their hands and stamped their feet as they had during shout worship of the past. They beat drums, jingled tambourines, and rang cymbals as they sang.

Gospel music also included call and response. While singing, someone would call out words of worship. Others would answer in song or with a form of "amen." Preachers also used this call and

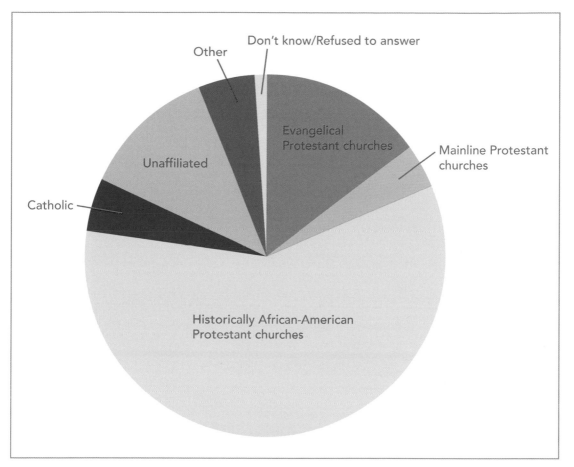

Other

Don't know/Refused to answer

Evangelical Protestant churches

Mainline Protestant churches

Unaffiliated

Catholic

Historically African-American Protestant churches

African Americans and Religion
The chart above shows what religious groups African Americans in the United States identified with in 2007. Gospel music arose in African-American Protestant churches. How does the information presented help you better understand the text?

response pattern during prayer. This was very much like expression used in Africa. Today many African-American churches still have a call and response in their worship services.

CHAPTER THREE

LITERATURE

African-American literature rose from slaves telling stories and folktales. Slaves recounted stories to entertain their listeners or to teach them moral lessons. Many slaves were not allowed to learn to read or write. But some found ways to learn. They began writing about their experience of slavery. African-American Frederick Douglass wrote about his life as a slave and his escape to freedom in the mid-

Contemporary writer Maya Angelou has captured the African-American experience in her books and poetry.

Children's Books

More and more books are being written for and about African-American children. They are written and illustrated by African Americans too. African-American Jacqueline Woodson is a well-known children's book author. Her book *Show Way* came out in 2005. The book tells the story of how slaves used quilts as maps to escape slavery. The book helps teach African-American children an important part of their culture and history.

1800s. His story was called *Narrative of the Life of Frederick Douglass, An American Slave.* It was well written and moving.

Writing for Civil Rights

Even after slavery ended, African Americans were treated poorly. They often faced violence at the hands of whites. African-American writers protested that treatment. A journalist named Ida B. Wells-Barnett was born in Mississippi in 1862. In 1892 Wells began writing newspaper editorials. She protested the lynching, or public hanging, of innocent African Americans in the South. She used her writing to call for the violence to end.

People treated African Americans as secondary. Much of the South was segregated. African Americans could not go to the same restaurants as whites. They sat in the backs of trolley cars while whites got to sit in the front. African Americans were frustrated that whites had not given them full freedom. In 1909 the National Association for the Advancement of Colored People (NAACP) was founded to try to change these things. The organization worked for equality of African Americans.

An African-American writer named W. E. B. Du Bois created the NAACP's magazine the *Crisis*. He edited the magazine from 1910 to 1934. African-American thinkers, writers, and poets published their writing in the magazine. The magazine showed the unique experiences of African Americans. The writings protested the unfair treatment they were receiving.

Harlem Renaissance

Around 1918 a literary and art movement started in Harlem, New York. It became known as the Harlem

Renaissance. African-American writers and artists wanted to break free from the stereotypes whites had put on them. They wanted to jumpstart a new awakening of African-American pride.

The Harlem Renaissance included a burst of African-American writing like no other time before. Langston Hughes and Zora Neale Hurston were two famous writers of the period. Their works showed the creative talent of African Americans. It also reflected their African-American heritage. The movement lasted until the mid-1930s. It is considered the most important literary period in African-American history.

More Powerful Writers

African-American writers kept telling their stories after the Harlem Renaissance. Richard Wright published his book *Black Boy* in 1945. It was the story of his childhood in the South. He wrote about the poverty and violence against African Americans there. Gwendolyn Brooks was a poet. In 1950 Brooks became the first African American to win a

Zora Neale Hurston was a key writer of the
Harlem Renaissance.

Pulitzer Prize for poetry. The Pulitzer Prize is one
of the highest awards a writer can receive. She
also published an autobiographical novel called

Maud Martha. This 1953 book is the story of an African-American woman growing up in Chicago, Illinois. Maud Martha has very black skin. She is made to feel ugly by whites and African Americans with lighter skin.

African-American Maya Angelou has written many novels and poems. One of her most famous books is *I Know Why the Caged Bird Sings.* It came out in 1969. It tells about her life growing up in Arkansas during segregation. The book is still widely read.

Today African-American writers address the African-American experience, as well as every topic available. And American literature is much richer for their contributions.

Zora Neale Hurston's essay "How It Feels to Be Colored Me" was published in 1928. In it she explains how she feels about her identity and being an African American:

> But I am not tragically colored. There is no great sorrow dammed up in my soul, nor lurking behind my eyes. I do not mind at all. I do not belong to the sobbing school of Negrohood who hold that nature somehow has given them a low-down dirty deal and whose feelings are all hurt about it. . . .
>
> I have no separate feeling about being an American citizen and colored. I am merely a fragment of the Great Soul that surges within the boundaries. My country, right or wrong.
>
> Sometimes, I feel discriminated against, but it does not make me angry. It merely astonishes me. How can any deny themselves the pleasure of my company? It's beyond me.

Source: Zora Neale Hurston. "How It Feels to Be Colored Me." The Best American Essays of the Century. Ed. Joyce Carol Oates. Boston: Houghton Mifflin, 2000. Print. 115–117.

What's the Big Idea?

Take a close look at this passage. What is Hurston's main point about how she feels to be an African American? Pick out two details she uses to make this point. How does this text help you better understand the Harlem Renaissance and its focus on African-American pride?

CHAPTER FOUR

MUSIC

As slaves toiled in southern fields, they called out to each other as they had in Africa. One slave called and another slave answered. Their calls might be of sorrow, hunger, or loneliness. Slaves turned their calls and cries into songs.

Religious Music

Slaves sang religious songs called spirituals. These songs expressed their yearning to be free and for

Enslaved African Americans sang while working in the fields.

Blues musicians often play the guitar.

better days to come. One of the best-known spirituals
is "Swing Low, Sweet Chariot." This song talks about
Heaven being a home. It is a place where slaves will
be free to rest. Slaves sang spirituals while working in
the fields.

Blues

After slavery ended in 1865, blues music began developing. Blues music grew out of the work songs slaves had sung in the fields. Blues music developed in the rural Mississippi Delta. After the Civil War ended in 1865, the United States began building a coast-to-coast railroad. Blues singers were fascinated by the railroad. They imagined riding off to a new place and leaving their troubles behind them.

The music blues singers sang was sad. They wailed about the new problems that freedom brought them. They might not have homes or jobs. Musicians also sang about love and loneliness. A singer strummed along on his guitar or played his harmonica between singing.

Ragtime

During the late 1800s, ragtime music developed in a few cities, including New Orleans. Its main characteristic was its ragged rhythm. Its rhythm was off the main beat. People liked to dance to the music. The music started losing popularity around 1920.

Louis Armstrong made jazz popular throughout the United States.

Jazz

During the late 1800s, musicians in New Orleans, Louisiana, began playing a new kind of music. It was called jazz. This new type of music was different from the blues. Instead of one musician playing a guitar, a whole band played. And the music was faster and more upbeat than blues had been.

Louis Armstrong was born in New Orleans in 1901. Armstrong started out playing jazz for white people on a Mississippi River boat. They loved his music. During the 1960s, an African American named John Coltrane was known as the angry jazz man. While other African Americans protested their unfair treatment with words, Coltrane rebelled through his music. In this way, music captured the experiences of African Americans.

Hip-Hop

In the 1970s, hip-hop music was developing. It was a new style of music that included rapping lyrics that rhymed. Music usually played in the background of the raps.

Hip-Hop's African Ties

Hip-hop reflects African culture. It is a bit like an African drummer who played his music and shouted to the dancers circling him. Hip-hop uses a disc jockey, or DJ, who plays music and calls out to listeners. It also has break dancing. This is a type of acrobatic dancing with headstands and tumbling. Break dancing is like African martial arts with its twirling and headstands.

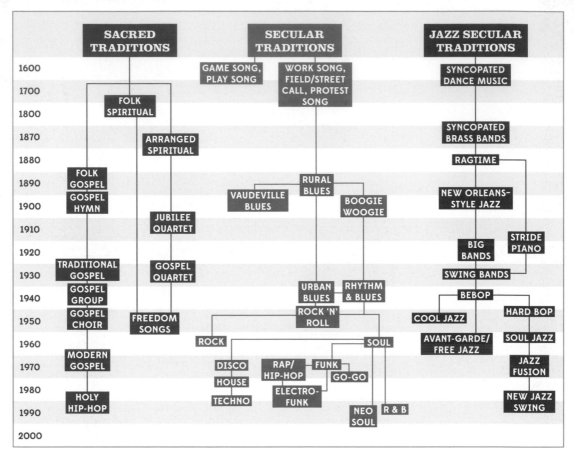

Development of African-American Music

The timeline shows the development of African-American sacred and secular music. Sacred music is religious. Secular music is not religious. How is this chart similar to what you have learned in this chapter? How is it different? How does this timeline help you better understand African-American music?

The raps were African-American storytelling. They revealed the challenges young African Americans faced. Lyrics often focused on being poor, growing

Kanye West and Jay Z are influential African-American hip-hop artists.

up with single mothers, or dropping out of school. The rappers also mentioned the struggle of growing up with drugs or gangs in their neighborhoods.

In 1979 the music group Sugarhill Gang released a 15-minute song called "Rapper's Delight." The song became very popular. Hip-hop music took off. Today hip-hop artists are well known in the music world. Jay Z is a famous rapper who has sold millions of albums. African Americans relate to his music. But his popularity goes beyond the African-American community. He is one of the biggest superstars in the world. Hip-hop started off as a unique part of African-American culture. It continues to be popular around the world today.

The hip-hop songs below by rappers Jay Z and 2Pac discuss the challenges some African-American youth face:

"No Hook" by Jay Z

Poor me, dad was gone . . .

Guidance? I never had that, streets was my second home

Welcomed me with open arms provided a place to crash at

A place to study math at, matter of fact, I learned it all

Source: Jay Z. American Gangster. *Rock-A-Fella Records, 2007. CD.*

"Dear Mama" by 2Pac

When I was young, me and my mama had beef

Seventeen years old kicked out on the streets . . .

Suspended from school; and scared to go home, I was a fool

With the big boys breaking all the rules

Source: 2Pac. Me Against the World. *Interscope Records, 1995. CD.*

Nice View

What is the point of view of each rapper? Write a short essay comparing the two rappers' points of view.

CHAPTER FIVE

FILM, TELEVISION, AND THEATER

In the decades after slavery, African Americans continued to struggle with severe racism and prejudice. This could be seen in how they were portrayed on screen. In early films, African Americans were often shown as lazy. A comedian named Lincoln Perry was the first African-American movie star. He acted in many movies in the mid-1930s. He played

Lincoln Perry, left, often played characters based on racial stereotypes.

a character who was lazy and tried to get out of doing work.

Awarded but Still Segregated

African Americans acted in early films. But their true experiences were not shown. At this time, African Americans could only get small roles that were often stereotypical. African-American women played maids or mammies. A mammy was an African-American nurse or servant to white children. African-American men played servants or butlers.

In 1939 African-American actress Hattie McDaniel played a role as a mammy. The new film was about the Civil War. It was called *Gone with the Wind*. McDaniel became the first African American

August Wilson, Playwright

August Wilson was born in 1945. He was a very talented playwright. Wilson quit school at age 15 when a teacher accused him of copying someone else's work. The teacher could not believe an African-American boy could write so well. Wilson grew up to win two Pulitzer Prizes for his plays.

Even though Hattie McDaniel, *right*, won an Academy Award, she still faced discrimination by the film industry.

to win an Academy Award. She won Best Actress in a Supporting Role. The premiere of the movie was shown in Atlanta, Georgia. During this time, the South was segregated. The theater was for whites only. McDaniel refused to go to the premiere because she knew she would not be allowed in the theater.

The ceremony for the awards was in 1940 in Los Angeles, California. McDaniel was not allowed to sit with her white costars. She had to sit at a separate table in the back of the room. Even though she won, McDaniel was kept separate from the white actors because of discrimination.

Lorraine Hansberry wrote about the experiences of her own family in *A Raisin in the Sun*.

A Raisin in the Sun

Some filmmakers and playwrights wanted to show what life was really like for African Americans. In 1959 Lorraine Hansberry's play *A Raisin in the Sun* was performed on Broadway in New York. It was the first time a play by an African-American woman had been performed there.

In the play, an African-American family living in Chicago is trying to improve their lives. The family wants to move out of their apartment and buy a house. But white people do not want them living next door. In 1961 the play became a movie. People around the country got to see a true example of African-American life.

Roles Keep Improving

Gradually audiences began to see more true-to-life African-American characters on screen. In 1967 African-American Sidney Poitier acted in the film *Guess Who's Coming to Dinner*. He played an intelligent doctor.

In the 1980s, African-American comedian Bill

Bad Experience into Hit TV Show

Actor and comedian Chris Rock was born in 1965. He attended a nearly all-white school in Brooklyn, New York. White kids beat Rock up. They called him terrible names. He dropped out of school in tenth grade. Rock turned the sad experience into comedy. In 2005 he created a television series called *Everybody Hates Chris*. It was based on his childhood.

Denzel Washington was the second African-American man to win Best Actor in a Leading Role.

Cosby played a father in a new show on television. *The Cosby Show* was about an African-American family. The father was a doctor. The mother was a successful lawyer. It was one of the first television shows to focus on an African-American family.

Winning Academy Awards

By the 1970s, more African Americans were getting leading roles in movies. In 2002 two African

Americans won the film industry's highest honors. Denzel Washington won the Academy Award for Best Actor in a Leading Role. Halle Berry won the Academy Award for Best Actress. This was the first time an African-American woman won this award. It was also the first year African Americans had won both awards for leading roles. Today African Americans contribute at all levels of making films and television shows, and to all other forms of cultural expression.

FURTHER EVIDENCE

Chapter Five discusses African Americans in film and television. What is one of the chapter's main points? What evidence is there in this chapter to support that point? Go to the website below to learn more about the history of African Americans in film. Find a quote from the website that supports the chapter's main point. Does the quote support an existing piece of evidence in the chapter? Or does it add a new one?

Representations of African Americans in Film
www.mycorelibrary.com/african-american-culture

IMPORTANT DATES

1619

The first African slaves arrive in the British colonies of the present-day United States.

1865

Slavery is outlawed in the United States.

1892

Ida B. Wells-Barnett begins writing newspaper articles protesting the lynching of African Americans.

1928

Zora Neale Hurston's "How It Feels to Be Colored Me" is published.

1940

Hattie McDaniel is the first African American to win an Academy Award.

1950

Gwendolyn Brooks becomes the first African American to win a Pulitzer Prize for poetry.

1896

Gospel music begins replacing spirituals in religious music.

1910

W. E. B. Du Bois begins editing the *Crisis*.

1918

The Harlem Renaissance starts in Harlem, New York.

1969

Maya Angelou's *I Know Why the Caged Bird Sings* is published.

1979

Hip-hop music gains popularity after Sugarhill Gang releases "Rapper's Delight."

2002

Halle Berry and Denzel Washington win Academy Awards for leading roles.

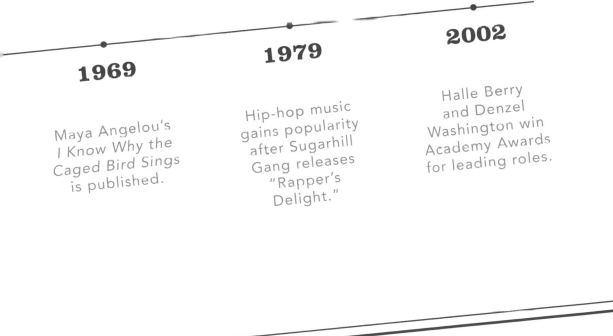

STOP AND THINK

You Are There

Chapter Four explains that blues musicians sang a lot about sorrow and hard times. Imagine you are a boy or girl watching a blues singer in your town when blues was just developing. What is the musician like? What is the musician singing about? What does the music make you feel and think about?

Tell the Tale

Chapter Two mentions that slaves sang spirituals while they worked in the fields. Write 200 words that tell the story of slaves singing while they worked. Describe how the people's voices sound. Are they hopeful or sad? Be sure to set the scene, develop a sequence of events, and offer a conclusion.

Say What?

Reading about African-American culture can introduce new vocabulary words. Find five words in this book that you've never heard before. Use a dictionary to look up what they mean. Then write the meanings in your own words. Use each word in a new sentence.

Surprise Me

Chapter Four discusses how African-American music developed. The development of different genres of music can be interesting and surprising. After reading this book, what two or three facts about African-American music did you find most surprising? Write a few sentences about each fact.

GLOSSARY

blues
a type of music developed by African Americans that is about life's challenges

culture
the way of life, customs, beliefs, and traditions of a group of people

hip-hop
a type of music developed by African Americans that includes rap

hymn
a song that praises God

jazz
a type of music developed by African Americans that is lively and does not follow written notes

literary
relating to literature

lyrics
the words of a song

prejudice
hatred or unfair treatment due to having fixed opinions about a group of people

renaissance
a period of much artistic or intellectual activity

segregate
to involuntarily separate or keep people apart from another group

spiritual
a type of religious music developed by African Americans during the time of slavery

LEARN MORE

Books

Mangrum, Allison. *African American Writers Who Inspired Change*. Brea, CA: Ballard & Tighe, 2006.

Weinstein, Muriel Harris. *Play, Louis, Play!: The True Story of a Boy and His Horn*. New York: Bloomsbury Books for Young Readers, 2010.

Websites

To learn more about African-American History, visit **booklinks.abdopublishing.com**. These links are routinely monitored and updated to provide the most current information available. Visit **www.mycorelibrary.com** for free additional tools for teachers and students.

INDEX

ABOUT THE AUTHOR

Darice Bailer is the author of many books for young readers. She was a journalist earlier in her career, and her articles have appeared in the *New York Times.* She lives with her husband in Connecticut.